A cut-a[...]
a Cross[...]

Car Deck

Inner Passeng[...]

Propulsion Units (4)

Lifting Fan Intakes

Control Cabin

Ventilators

Unloading Ramp

A Ladybird Book
Series 654

The hovercraft is a relatively new form of transport — quite different from any wheeled vehicle, ship or aeroplane — yet combining many of the capabilities of all three.

The main features of hovercraft design and their method of operation are described in this book with superb colour illustrations and a text which is easy to understand. Modern air cushion vehicles are illustrated as are some other applications of the air cushion principle.

We wish to acknowledge the assistance of
THE BRITISH HOVERCRAFT CORPORATION
when preparing this book.

'How it works'
THE
HOVERCRAFT

by E. S. HAYDEN
with illustrations by B. H. ROBINSON

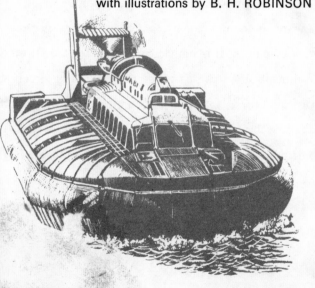

Publishers : Wills & Hepworth Ltd Loughborough

First published 1969   ©   *Printed in England*

How it works – the Hovercraft

The hovercraft is an entirely new form of transport, and is quite different from any wheeled vehicle, ship or aeroplane. However, the hovercraft combines many of the capabilities of all three; it can carry heavy loads over land, it can operate on the sea and it is airborne in operation.

Hovercraft hover, or ride, on a cushion of air and so they are sometimes called *air cushion vehicles* or *ground effect* machines. If a vehicle can be made to float on a cushion of air, it can easily be moved in any direction by a small force. However, it could easily be moved off its course by wind or waves, so an accurate system of control is needed to move it from place to place safely. Generally, a hovercraft has no physical contact with the surface over which it is travelling, so the controls must be aerodynamic—rather like aircraft controls.

An illustration of an SRN6, which is now in regular passenger-carrying service, is shown on the opposite page. The main features of its design and their method of operation are described in the following pages.

7214 0231 3

Early experiments: High pressure air pads

Over the years, two separate lines of thought developed regarding the application of the 'hover' principle to vehicles. One envisaged the support of a vehicle on '*pads*' of *high*-pressure air, the other envisaged its support on a '*cushion*' of *low*-pressure air.

It was at first thought that pads of high-pressure air could possibly replace wheels, the wheels of, say, a motor car. However, two main difficulties became apparent. The first was that with pads of high-pressure air, it proved difficult and wasteful of power to lift the car high enough for it to travel over any but the smoothest surface. The second difficulty was that of propulsion: as soon as physical contact with the ground was severed, a new method of propulsion had to be devised to replace that usually supplied by the wheels.

Because of these problems, the hover*car* concept has tended to be confined to the hovertrain. Rails provide an ideal smooth surface for the high-pressure air pads, and also overcome the problem of steering. The vehicle is then ideally suited for propulsion by some form of aero engine or some type of electrical induction motor.

Diagrams on the opposite page show the simple high-pressure air pad, and the type of air pad that could be used for hovertrains.

High-Pressure Air Input

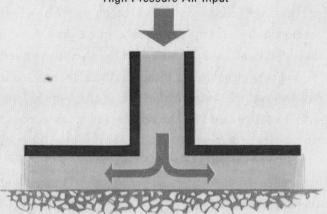

SIMPLE AIR PAD

High-Pressure Air Input

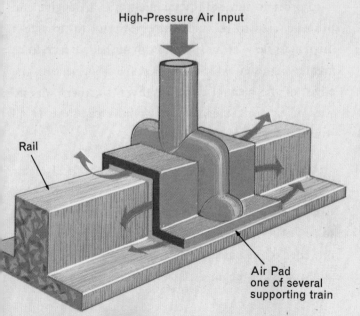

Rail

Air Pad
one of several
supporting train

HOVERTRAIN AIR PAD

The air-cushion – or 'plenum chamber'

The idea of supporting a vehicle on a *cushion* of air developed from early attempts at producing vertical take-off aircraft, and also the wish to increase the speed of boats by feeding air beneath them to ease their passage over the water. Propellers, in the form of fans, were used to provide 'lift' by keeping full of low-pressure air a cavity underneath the craft. The air lifted the craft and escaped around the edges. This cavity, or chamber, was called a 'plenum' chamber from the Latin word 'plenum', meaning 'full'.

In order to successfully maintain lift, the engine and propeller had to be sufficiently powerful to provide a 'high mass flow' of air. The flow of air had, in fact, to be greater than that which could escape from beneath the edges of the plenum chamber. Even so, there was no way of ensuring that the air would escape evenly all round the edge of the chamber.

A vehicle resting on a plenum chamber full of air was rather like you sitting on a large, very soft, rubber ball—the slightest state of unbalance could cause you to roll off. The slightest state of unbalance could cause one edge of the plenum chamber to dig into the ground, whilst most of the air escaped from the other side.

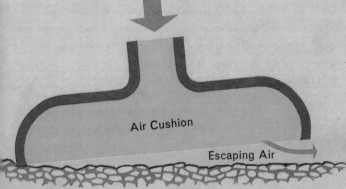

High Mass Flow of Air

Air Cushion

Escaping Air

OPEN PLENUM CHAMBER IN STATE OF UNBALANCE

The momentum curtain

The plenum chamber type of hovercraft showed the most promise of successful development, but it had problems of stability and required tremendous power to maintain a reasonable hover height. Some of the early types used high-pressure air jets to balance, or 'trim', the craft, and these were controlled from the cabin. However, stability of the hovercraft on its cushion of air still remained a real problem.

To solve these problems, a plenum chamber with a *momentum curtain* was developed. The plenum chamber was almost filled with a box-like structure, thereby forming a slot round the plenum chamber wall and which was, of course, open at the bottom edge. A curtain of flowing air, which inclined inwards and maintained the air-cushion, could therefore be created.

This arrangement achieved higher heights with less power. It also solved the stability problem, as the air flow to the momentum curtain could be controlled by the commander, and he could maintain balance of the craft quite easily. Later, the bottom edge was closed and slots provided for the passage of air. (See top drawing, Page 13.)

The box structure in the plenum chamber had the added advantage that it could be made watertight, and thereby form a *buoyancy tank* on which a hovercraft could float when at rest on water.

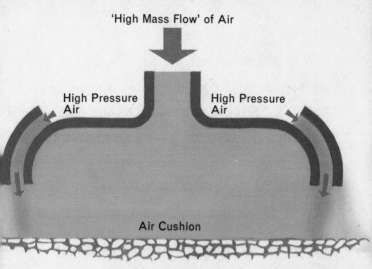

EARLY OPEN PLENUM CHAMBER WITH H.P. AIR JETS TO BALANCE THE CRAFT

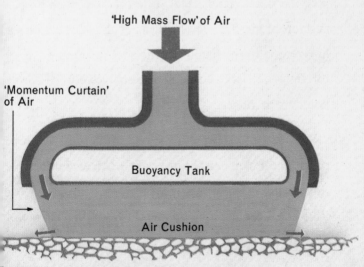

SIMPLE SLOTTED PLENUM CHAMBER WITH 'MOMENTUM CURTAIN'

Skirts

Workable hovercraft can be built using a plenum chamber employing the momentum curtain technique. In fact, the first one to cross the English Channel used this system. However, the hover height was still too low unless great, and uneconomical, power was used. Simple obstacles such as quite small waves, or a tide-formed ridge of shingle on a beach, could prove inconvenient.

These problems led to the development of the 'skirt'. This is a shaped, flexible skirt fitted below the bottom edges of the plenum chamber slot. As the hovercraft lifts, the skirt extends below it to retain a much deeper cushion of air. The development of the skirt enables a hovercraft to maintain its normal operating speed through quite large waves. It also enables it to pass over boulders or ridges.

The skirt of a hovercraft is one of its most sensitive parts. The design must be just right, or an uncomfortable ride results. Also, excessive wear of the skirt can occur if its edges are flapping up and down on the surface of the sea.

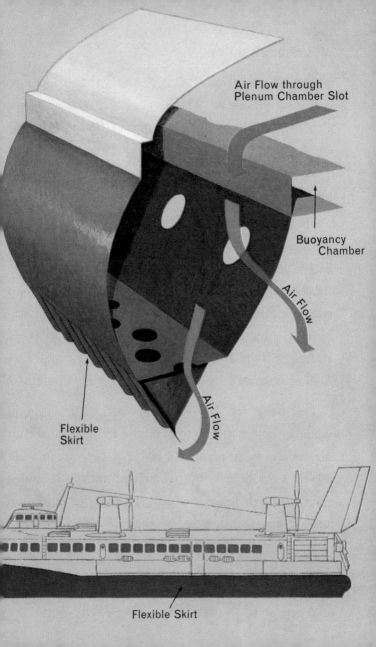

Air Flow through
Plenum Chamber Slot

Buoyancy
Chamber

Air Flow

Air Flow

Flexible
Skirt

Flexible Skirt

Main construction

As with any vehicle, fuel is wasted when moving any unnecessary weight. This is particularly true of an airborne vehicle, and therefore aircraft techniques of construction are used in the building of hovercraft. This ensures maximum possible strength with the least possible weight.

The basic structure of the hovercraft is a flat-topped plenum chamber of oval or rectangular shape, and the cabin, engine, control gear and plenum chamber air intake are all fitted above the floor formed by the top of the plenum chamber. With single-engined vehicles, the air intake and engine are at the rear, and the passenger or freight compartment is forward. The air intake is as high as possible to avoid the entry of spray and dust.

The buoyancy tank is fitted within the plenum chamber so that there is a space over the top of it and an air slot around its edges. The whole of the space through which the cushion air flows is finished with flush-headed rivets, smooth bends and smooth edges to ensure an uninterrupted air flow and maximum cushion efficiency.

A system of control rudders and tail-planes is mounted at the extreme rear.

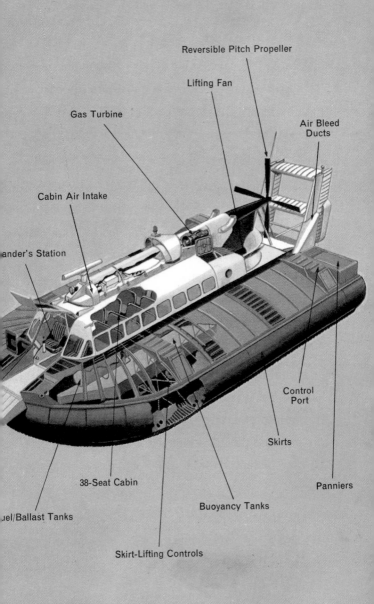

Reversible Pitch Propeller

Lifting Fan

Gas Turbine

Air Bleed Ducts

Cabin Air Intake

ander's Station

Control Port

Skirts

38-Seat Cabin

Panniers

Buoyancy Tanks

uel/Ballast Tanks

Skirt-Lifting Controls

The lift fan

Although it is necessary to raise the chamber pressure only a little above atmospheric pressure in order to lift the hovercraft, this is not easy to do. Great care has to be taken to design smooth air ducts with as few bends as possible, and the lift fans must be very efficient.

The lifting fan used with smaller momentum curtain hovercraft is about seven or eight feet in diameter and twelve to eighteen inches deep. Such a fan requires tremendous power to drive it and uses most of the power developed by the engine. The size of a lift fan of the British Railways cross-Channel hovercraft can be judged by the illustration opposite. It is twelve-bladed and eleven feet, six inches in diameter.

The design of the lifting fan is very carefully considered, for it is one of the most important parts of the hovercraft. Not only must it be very efficient in pumping air into the plenum chamber, but it must be very accurately balanced or it could shake the hovercraft to pieces.

The shaft of the fan is mounted vertically (see page 21) and air is forced into the plenum chamber at right angles to the axis of rotation.

Lifting power

Let us imagine a hovercraft which, complete with crew, fuel and load, weighs 4,000 pounds (lbs.), and is 20 feet (ft.) long and 10 ft. wide. Its area would be 20 ft. $\times$ 10 ft. = 200 square (sq.) ft. If the craft is to hover, the pressure of air forming the cushion must be approximately 4,000 lbs. This represents 20 lbs. per sq. ft.

It is worth noting how little pressure—only 20 lbs. per sq. ft.—is required to lift the hovercraft.

From experience with the hovercraft which have been developed, it is possible to make some simple formulae. One of these is that a cushion pressure of 20 lbs. per sq. ft. can be maintained by 4 horsepower for each sq. ft. of curtain area. Curtain area is its length times its height.

A hovercraft 20 ft. long by 10 ft. wide would have a curtain length of 60 ft.—twice the length plus twice the width. If we want it to hover one foot high we would need sufficient power to provide a curtain of 60 $\times$ 1 sq. ft. At 4 horsepower per sq. ft. we would need 240 horsepower for lift alone.

18

$20 \times 10 = 200$ square feet area

$$\frac{4{,}000 \text{ pounds weight}}{200 \text{ sq. ft. area}} = \frac{20 \text{ pounds per sq. ft. cushion}}{\text{pressure required to lift craft}}$$

Weight - 4000 pounds

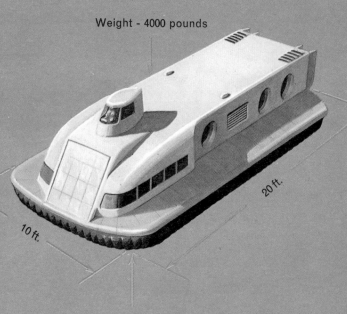

10 ft.

20 ft.

Hoverheight - 1 foot

$20 + 20 + 10 + 10 = 60$ feet circumference of curtain

At a hover height of 1 foot, 60 square feet of curtain must be maintained at 4 horsepower per square foot

60×4 240 horsepower required to maintain lift alone

The propeller

The propeller used to drive the hovercraft along is usually an aircraft type with variable pitch blades. As you will see from the diagram opposite, its speed of rotation must remain fixed to that of the engine and the lift fan. This is because the amount of lift required is the all-important factor which decides the engine speed, so the amount of propulsion which the propellers provide must be obtained by varying the propeller pitch. This system is termed 'integrated lift/propulsion'. Hovercraft having more than one lift fan and propeller generally have a separate engine for each fan-and-propeller unit.

The propellers used on hovercraft are four-bladed and about nine feet in diameter on the smaller craft. The four propellers on the SRN4 cross-Channel hovercraft are four-bladed and nineteen feet in diameter. The pylons on which they are mounted can be swivelled to change the direction of thrust. Engines, propellers, pylons and all gearboxes can be removed for overhaul without disturbing the lift fans or the main structure.

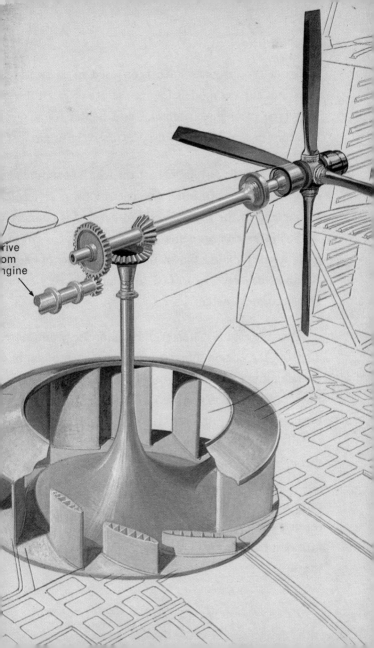

rive
om
ngine

The engine

Piston type engines have been used in early hover craft, but current models favour the use of gas turbines. This type of engine is smaller and lighter for a given horsepower and has been used extensively in aircraft.

The engine has a main shaft on which is mounted a compressor and a turbine. A starter motor is connected to one end of the shaft and the other end is connected to the lift fan and propeller gearboxes. Both compressor and turbine look like fans with a large number of blades. Because they revolve so fast they must be very strong and accurately made.

When the engine is started, the compressor compresses air from the engine intakes and pushes it into combustion chambers mounted around the engine. Fuel, either low grade petrol or kerosene, is squirted into the combustion chambers and ignited. The compressed air then rapidly expands as it is heated and forces its way out through the turbine to the exhaust. As the gas pressure rises, the turbine speeds up, thereby driving the compressor faster. The engine speed increases until it reaches the engine's normal operating speed of around fifteen to twenty thousand revolutions per minute (r.p.m.).

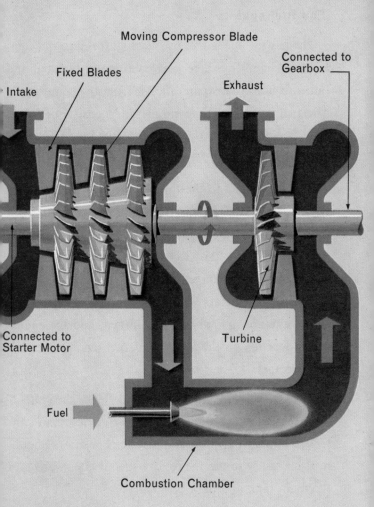

SIMPLIFIED DIAGRAM OF GAS TURBINE ENGINE

The fuel system

The gas turbine works by injecting fuel into the combustion chamber, where it is continuously ignited and burnt to heat and expand the air from the compressor. The fuel system is quite simple and consists of a fuel tank, a pump, a throttle valve and as many injectors as there are combustion chambers.

Fuel is pumped to the throttle valve by means of an electrically driven pump. If the throttle is closed, no fuel passes to the engine. As the twist grip throttle control is turned, the electrically driven throttle-valve opens and fuel is pumped through the injectors into the combustion chambers. The throttle opens in proportion to the amount the twist grip is turned, and the engine speed depends on the amount of fuel passing through the injectors.

Reserve fuel may also be used to balance the craft. If it is, the balance is adjusted by an electric pump controlled by a switch at the commander's position. Should it be necessary to use the reserve fuel, it is pumped into the main tank and used normally.

The amount of fuel available in the tanks is shown on indicators at the commander's position.

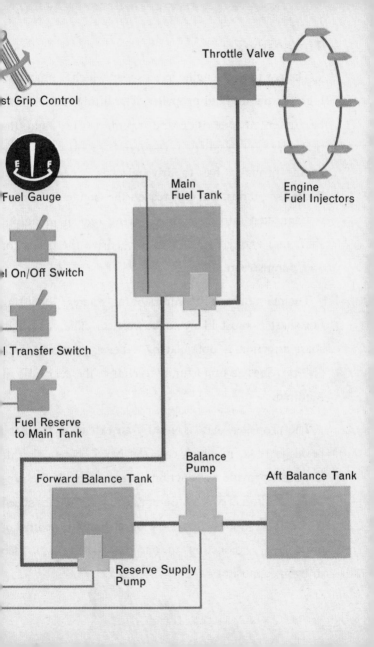

The gearbox

The gas turbine engine has a speed which is much too high for the fan and propeller. The lifting fan needs to be driven at one thousand r.p.m. or less and the propeller at about two thousand r.p.m. Also, the engine probably has to drive electric generators and hydraulic pumps. For this reason the engine drive shaft is connected into a gearbox having one main output shaft and enough smaller ones to drive the generator and pumps required.

The main drive shaft is horizontal, whereas the lifting fan shaft is most likely to be vertical. The change in shaft direction is obtained by a bevel gearbox, which also provides an opportunity to change the gear ratio, if required.

The propeller shaft is usually an extension from the bevel gearbox, in which case the bevel gear to the lift fan must provide a reduction in gear ratio. If the propeller rotation is two thousand r.p.m. when engine speed is twenty thousand r.p.m., the bevel gear to the lift fan must give a reduction to one thousand r.p.m. (see drawing opposite).

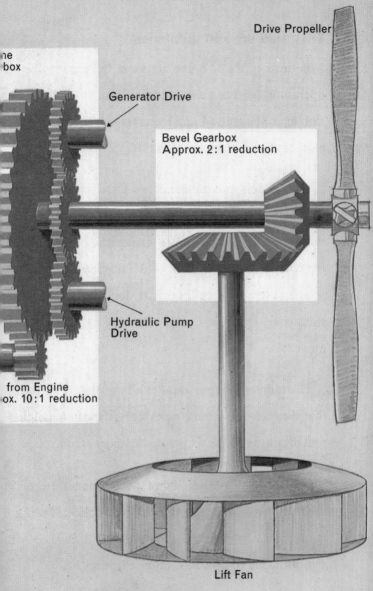

Drive Propeller

Generator Drive

Bevel Gearbox
Approx. 2:1 reduction

...ne
...box

Hydraulic Pump
Drive

from Engine
...ox. 10:1 reduction

Lift Fan

PRINCIPLE OF GEAR REDUCTION

Fins, rudders and tailplanes

Because of the airborne nature of hovercraft when in operation, most of them use stabilizing fins and rudders similar to the conventional aircraft pattern. Some types also have one or more tailplanes.

The rudders and tailplanes are fitted as near the rear end of the hovercraft as is practicable, in order to have the maximum control effect. Generally, they look very big compared with the size of the hovercraft. This is to provide the necessary control at slow speeds, and when stationary, from the thrust provided by the propeller alone.

The tailplanes are normally 'all-moving'. This means that they have no separate elevators, the whole tailplane moving in response to the commander's control.

Fins, rudders and tailplanes are all manufactured in accordance with standard aircraft practice. They are made light and strong of light alloy and finished with smooth skins to give maximum efficiency.

Controlling the hovercraft

Basically, hovercraft require lift and propulsion. Lift is entirely dependent on the speed of the engine driving the lift fan. Control of lift is obtained by opening and closing the engine throttle. Usually, the throttle control is a twist-grip type control on a lever to one side of the commander. The lever usually controls the pitch of the propeller. Moving the lever forward moves the hovercraft forward at increasing speed. Pulling it back slows down and, if pulled far enough, reverses the hovercraft.

Directional control is provided by aircraft type rudder pedals which control the rudders. Sometimes the propeller pylons are made to swivel to assist steering. Also, small plenum chamber bleed jets may be used at the corners of the hovercraft to assist steering.

Movement of the control lever operates a motor in the propeller boss to move the propeller blade pitch. The blades move from zero pitch (zero thrust) to coarse pitch. The coarser the pitch of the blades the faster the hovercraft moves. Reverse pitch on the blades moves the craft backwards.

Controls vary in different hovercraft but they all use the same principles of operation.

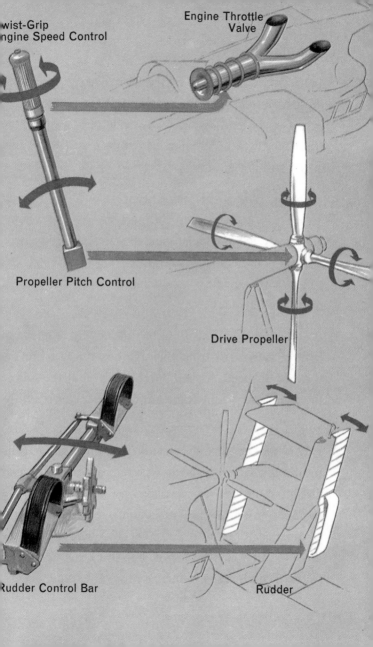

Auxiliary controls

The most important of these auxiliary controls are those used to balance the hovercraft. Because the freight or passenger load may vary in weight and position, the whole craft must be balanced before it will lift evenly on its cushion of air.

One method of obtaining static balance is to pump water ballast forwards or aft to trim the craft. Some hovercraft now use fuel instead of water, and so provide a reserve fuel supply. Fuel transfer to achieve balance is controlled by pumps responding to switches operated by the commander.

Some hovercraft also use the all-moving tailplane to control balance or trim when the hovercraft is moving forward at speed. A small lever or wheel at the side of the commander adjusts the tailplane and, consequently, the trim.

It is also possible to control the momentum curtain to tilt the hovercraft and assist it to move in a particular direction. This effect is assisted by lifting the skirt at the appropriate point. The action is controlled by the commander's joystick and the craft will tilt in the direction in which he moves it. Tilting the hovercraft forward can be used to increase forward speed.

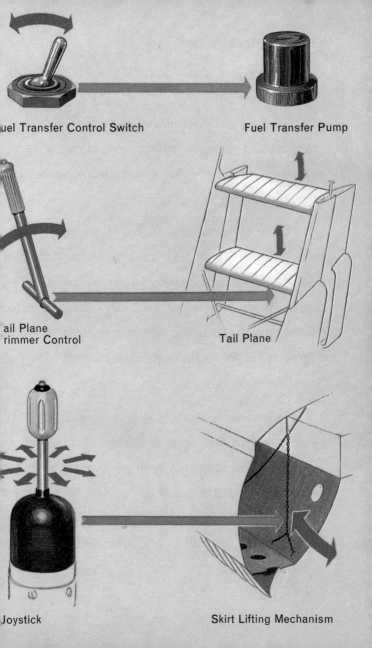

uel Transfer Control Switch

Fuel Transfer Pump

ail Plane
rimmer Control

Tail Plane

Joystick

Skirt Lifting Mechanism

The electrical system

Electrical power is used to start the engine and ignite the fuel driving the engine. The lights, radio, radar equipment and many instruments also require electricity. Electrical systems also offer a convenient, efficient method of control of other systems where mechanical control might not be practicable.

For all of these reasons, modern vehicles rely heavily on their supply of electricity. The supply is first obtained from a generator which charges a battery to maintain a supply when the engine is stopped. A voltage regulator ensures that the battery is not over or under charged. A ground supply socket enables an external supply to be connected during servicing.

The generator and battery supply the electricity. All electrical circuits use electricity either from the battery alone when the engine is stopped, or from the generator and battery when the engine is running. The diagram on the opposite page shows a simplified electrical system. All of the circuits are controlled by switches at the commander's position.

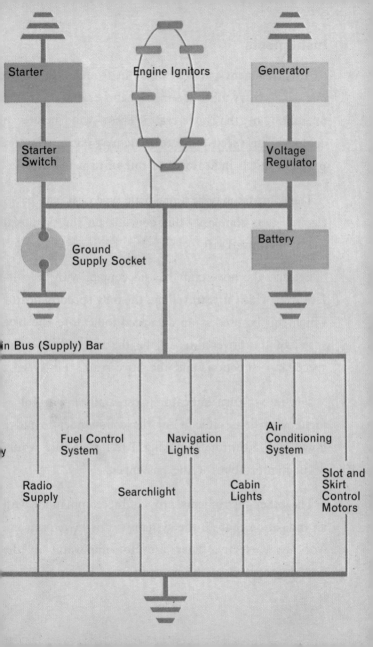

Instruments

An instrument panel is fitted in front of the commander to carry all of the instruments essential for safe operation of the hovercraft. These will include a compass, air speed indicator, engine r.p.m. indicator, propeller pitch indicator and rate-of-turn indicator.

The compass may be a magnetic type or it may be an electric gyro compass—this depends on the proposed use of the hovercraft.

Because the hovercraft has no contact with the surface over which it is travelling, the only speed indicator which can be used is an air speed indicator. The true speed of the hovercraft will be the sum of the wind speed and direction, and the hovercraft's air speed.

The rate-of-turn indicator is especially important at night when it is difficult for the commander to judge how 'tight' a turn he is making. Too tight a turn would be uncomfortable for the passengers.

The other instruments provide the commander with an indication that all the systems in the hovercraft are working correctly. They are not important in the hovering control of the hovercraft.

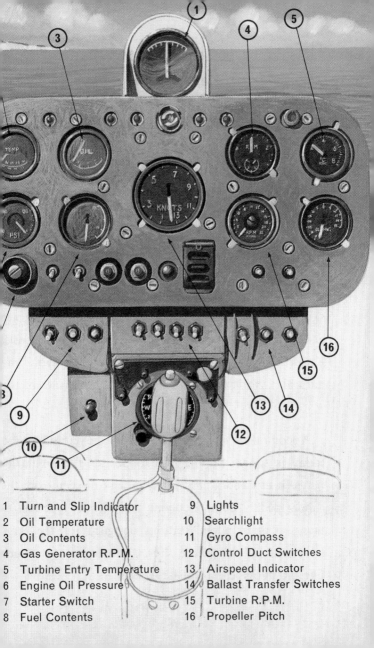

1	Turn and Slip Indicator	9	Lights
2	Oil Temperature	10	Searchlight
3	Oil Contents	11	Gyro Compass
4	Gas Generator R.P.M.	12	Control Duct Switches
5	Turbine Entry Temperature	13	Airspeed Indicator
6	Engine Oil Pressure	14	Ballast Transfer Switches
7	Starter Switch	15	Turbine R.P.M.
8	Fuel Contents	16	Propeller Pitch

The commander's station

Because of the unique nature of the hovercraft, there has been some uncertainty as to what title should be given to the person controlling a hovercraft and what qualifications are required. Generally, they are now called commanders, some of them being ex-aircraft pilots.

Hovercraft in use today are, generally, used more over the sea than elsewhere. Consequently, the commander needs to be a person combining many of the piloting skills of an aircraft pilot with the navigational skills of a sea captain. The controls of a hovercraft are aerodynamic, very much like an aircraft's controls. Knowledge of seamanship is necessary to avoid the natural hazards of the sea and to obey the rules of the sea.

A 'commander's station' typical of hovercraft in use today is shown on the page opposite. The similarity between this and a pilot's cockpit can be seen from the rudder pedals, control column and aircraft type instruments. Commanders' stations designed for the large hovercraft of the future show them to be very much like the pilots' cabins of large airliners.

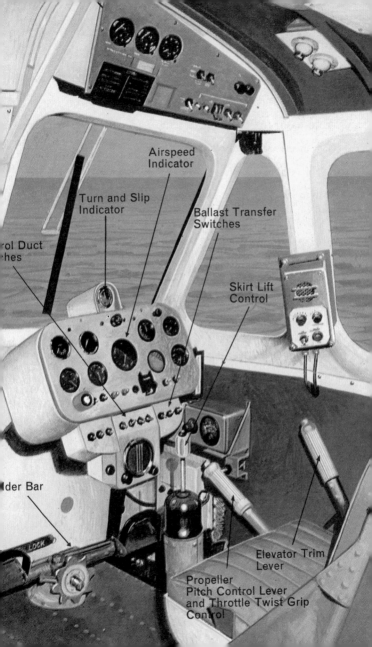

Turn and Slip
Indicator

Airspeed
Indicator

Ballast Transfer
Switches

rol Duct
hes

Skirt Lift
Control

der Bar

Elevator Trim
Lever

Propeller
Pitch Control Lever
and Throttle Twist Grip
Control

LOCK

The passenger cabin

The cabin is typical of the slower passenger aircraft, except that seat belts have not so far been considered necessary. Because the length of journeys made are at present quite short, the seats are like those in buses. The standard of passenger comfort will be improved to meet passengers' needs when hovercraft are developed for longer journeys.

The hovercraft produces considerable spray under certain conditions, so the windows are not designed to open, except in an emergency, and an air conditioning system is provided.

On smaller hovercraft, access to the cabin is by a door at the forward end of the cabin. This door folds forwards and down to provide a ramp. The commander's position is at the forward right-hand side of the cabin, and provision is made on the left-hand side for a navigator or radar operator.

Should an emergency occur, lifejackets are available under the seats. The windows are designed to be pushed outward to provide emergency exits. Also, inflatable life-rafts are carried.

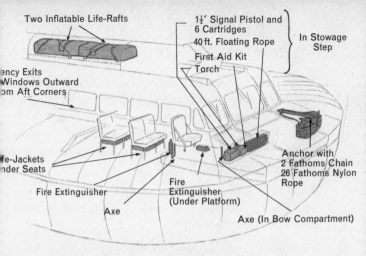

Two Inflatable Life-Rafts

1½" Signal Pistol and 6 Cartridges
40 ft. Floating Rope

In Stowage Step

First Aid Kit

Torch

ency Exits
Windows Outward
om Aft Corners

Anchor with
2 Fathoms Chain
26 Fathoms Nylon Rope

fe-Jackets
nder Seats

Fire Extinguisher

Axe

Fire Extinguisher
(Under Platform)

Axe (In Bow Compartment)

EMERGENCY EQUIPMENT AND EXITS

Hovercraft performance

The performance of a hovercraft is usually indicated by a detailed list which includes operating weight, speed and other factors which determine how best it can be used. For instance, the performance of hovercraft already in passenger service is roughly as shown in the following simplified list:

Mean operating weight (including craft, crew, half fuel load and three-quarters payload)	17,000 lb. (nearly 8 tons)
Maximum speed (knots=sea miles per hour)	about 60 knots
Service speed	about 50 knots
Turn radius at 40 knots	300–400 yards
Calm water range	about 200 miles
Obstacle clearance	3–4 feet
Maximum gradient	1 in 10

The main feature of the hovercraft is that it can achieve its performance over any kind of surface; water, swamp or rough land. The only limiting factors are obstacle height, gradient and the state of the sea. As mentioned, obstacle clearance is improved by the use of skirts. The maximum slope which can be climbed is mainly dependent upon the amount of 'control' power available. The picture on the opposite page shows a hovercraft shooting turbulent rapids in Malaysia, Borneo. This is typical of the hovercraft's ability to travel over any kind of surface.

Commercial operation

Not only can a hovercraft travel over any surface, but it also has the advantage of not requiring any special 'terminal' facilities. It can float alongside a pontoon or jetty—as more conventional ferries do—or it can hover up and settle on a beach. In fact, it can sit happily on any reasonable surface.

For this reason, the hovercraft has particular value as a freight or passenger carrier in swamp or jungle areas. No special preparation is necessary, other than the preparation of a clearway through trees, and the removal of any boulders too big for the hovercraft to ride over.

Although special terminal facilities are not required for the hovercraft when used as a ferry, they are necessary to ensure passenger comfort and efficiency in passenger and traffic 'flow'—thereby reducing the 'turn-round' time of the craft and making it more profitable. So far, hovercraft terminals in use seem to favour the use of slipways so that passengers can embark and disembark on dry land. Also, such an arrangement provides simple 'parking' of the hovercraft and easy access to it for servicing and refuelling.

Doubtless the large hovercraft of the future will require some special facilities, but they are not likely to be as expensive as docks, runways or motorways.

A giant crosses the English Channel

During August, 1968, British Rail commenced a cross-Channel service using the SRN4—a one hundred and sixty-five ton hovership suitable for all-the-year round services over open coastal water routes such as the English Channel, and capable of journeys up to one hundred nautical miles over waves as high as eight to twelve feet.

The hovership is designed to accommodate two hundred and fifty-four passengers and thirty cars, but an all-passenger version could provide over six hundred seats.

The car deck is in the centre of the craft, with large doors in the stern and a ramp in the bow to make it possible to drive-in and drive-off. On either side of the car deck are passenger saloons, equipped with comfortable seats for all passengers and with large windows extending the full length of the craft. The control cabin is above the car deck and is sited well forward to provide the three-man operating crew (commander, engineer and radar operator/navigator) with all-round visibility.

The SRN4 is powered by four Bristol Siddeley 'Marine Proteus' gas turbine engines, each one driving a variable pitch propeller mounted on a pylon. Interconnected with the propellers are four centrifugal fans to provide the cushion air. The craft is controlled by varying the propeller blade angles, and by swivelling the pylons to vary the direction of thrust. If one engine should fail, the craft can still proceed as a hovercraft on the remaining three. It is completely buoyant, and could move forward *on* the water with only one engine. Hovercraft speed into the wind is as high as fifty/sixty knots even with eight to ten feet waves.

Close relations – how they work

The air cushion principle is being applied to land and water craft which, because they are never completely airborne, do not strictly qualify as hovercraft. More correctly they are 'air lubricated' vehicles. It is felt that this book would be incomplete without some mention of them.

Because they do not sever contact with the surface over which they are travelling, they do not need to use aerodynamic control. Instead, they may use conventional land or water techniques.

For instance, a Land Rover has been developed which has sidewalls and a skirt to contain an air cushion sufficient to enable it to pass over swampland. Its wheels still provide traction and steering. A heavy load transporter has been designed which uses a large air pad to help support the load, but which still relies on wheels for traction and control.

A large variety of air lubricated boats have been developed. Some have sidewalls and skirts containing a cushion, others use a large number of air pads to provide air lubrication. In most cases they rely on water propellers and rudders for propulsion and control.

Yet another application of the air-cushion principle was the moving of a three hundred thousand gallon oil storage tank. This was floated on a cushion of air and moved three hundred and fifty yards to a new site.

Another close relation

A much smaller—though nevertheless important—development of the air-cushion principle has been its application to the lifting and moving of loads of up to five tons from one point to another inside factories, warehouses, aircraft and ships. For this purpose the 'hoverpallet' has been developed.

As can be seen in the illustration opposite, the hover-pallet consists of a load-carrying platform with a tubular handle and frame. Air for the air-cushion is supplied to four easily-removable assemblies underneath the platform. With the load in position, the control valve is opened until the load is airborne, when it can then be pushed, pulled or turned in any direction. When the desired position is reached, the control valve is closed and the load settles gently to the ground.

One of the advantages of using this method of moving heavy loads within buildings, aircraft or ships is that there is no danger whatever of smooth floors being scratched or damaged. Also, the high manoeuvrability in confined spaces is particularly valuable. The air-cushions spread the load sufficiently to make operation possible over weak floors which could not otherwise bear the concentrated axle weights of wheeled vehicles.

Series 654
A Ladybird 'How it works' Book